POETRY of PLACE

RIZZOLI
NEW YORK

New York Paris London Milan

POETRY OF PLACE

THE NEW ARCHITECTURE AND INTERIORS OF
McALPINE

Bobby McAlpine
WITH SUSAN SULLY

For many of us, the search for finding home is long and elusive. This book is dedicated to the tireless, fearless, reckless, and brave who jumped off a cliff of faith to build a place that, until then, existed only in their hearts. Lit by original magic, they developed an appetite for integrity and could not compromise their vision. I salute you cowboys and cowgirls of industry. With your invitation, we get to exercise and groom our own hearts and reshape the world into familiar chords.

CONTENTS

BEAUTY, TRUTH, AND LOVE

"Come let me love you," said the house. Some houses beckon to us this way. They are anthropomorphic and emotionally alive. Their character and soul exceed their parts. They have a voice and give us one as well, reminding us that we are loved lavishly and unreservedly, that we are free to get things wrong without fear of abandonment, that we are called to create our lives out of glorious individuality. This kind of beauty includes us. It feeds emotions we are starving for and captures feelings we know well.

Beauty is a place we love to go, a place where we exist at our best.

What our culture teaches us about beauty—its attributes and golden proportions—is different from what our hearts know, which is a more complex mix of attractions filled with flaws and contradictions. We love some of the most ridiculous-looking animals because they pull at some heartstring in us. True infectious beauty is not easily described as perfection—there is no doctrine for it. When the world does not look the way it should to our hearts, we need to create one that does. We all have an angel on one shoulder telling us to look at what's correct and not embarrass ourselves, and another,

that says to do anything we please as long as it's pertinent to our stories and helps us tell them.

In the youth of my practice, I developed an appetite for authenticity and correctness. I learned what was right in order to execute with full knowledge what was wrong—rules be damned. That's the difference between doctrine and emotional accuracy. Perhaps that's why I've come to think of Hollywood as our emotional architect. In classic movies, there is often a naivety with which their architectural settings are depicted. If you look at an old movie set in New England, the architecture of

the backdrop might have giant windowpanes and a quality of openness and gladness not possessed by the prim, white clapboard buildings that inspired it. It's not one-hundred percent correct, but emotionally it's spot-on. The designers may not have known better, but more likely they were following the story closely and doing whatever it took to tell it.

This is the power of wrong—of finding the courage to beg, borrow, and steal until you get the story right. It's the freedom to crossbreed things that have never met before but somehow embolden each other. Sometimes a bit of exaggeration is required to drive a point home. To hold on to the things that marked us and changed us forever, we may need to recast them as bigger, bolder, and more intense than they really were. As narrative devices go, exaggeration is a potent one, as long as it doesn't squash the subtlety and tender seasonings of great storytelling.

A brassy house viewed primarily as a trophy beats its chest so loudly you find it hard to get near. It demands your notice by shouting, as opposed to the one over in the corner that's somehow more attractive because it has a quiet knowing you want so much to have for yourself. A house like this doesn't tell the whole story at once—it reserves its most dramatic gestures for the final act. You begin dancing with it before you realize how wonderful it is. When at last you step out onto the terrace and look back, you discover something far grander than you could have imagined. The final thing you come to know is the greatest thing. It is the finale, the last big scene.

You see this in so many great stories where a character blossoms before your eyes over the short passage of a film or pages of a book. Sometimes the story is so big that it needs to be slowed, the lights dimmed, and a few things kept at bay until the moment of discovery is at hand. The devices that tell these stories—sequencing, the unveiling of secrets, and the revelation of magnificence—can be translated into architectural language and paced to create a forever memorable environment. The least glimpse inside—that's the enticement. It's that millisecond that invites you in, even if it's a flash.

I've often wondered why houses that are transparent also instill something favorable in me. Perhaps it's because the house is being honest and truthful about itself. It has gotten out of its own way enough to be clear hearted—clear to the core—and to show its intelligence. It's at rest because it has such an organized sense of self. What it delivers is not convoluted or veiled in misalignment. When you are there, you also find the possibility to come to rest. You can put your faith in a thing that is at peace with itself. This is the medicine of being in the right environment.

A place that is prepared for you is one that has made room for you—it reserves space where you can find some quiet and untangle and organize yourself. It becomes your new outer being. You shape it and it shapes you. Once you've found that, you can wander more freely, naked amongst the parts of yourself. When the right walls come up around you, your own walls dissolve.

"Come let me love you," said the house. Good architecture says subtly—if you should wander, if you should wonder, if you are loved, if you are seen—come back to me. I am a constant in your life. I'll say this again and again until you hear it, until you own it, until you don't need me anymore, until you are structured the same, until you know your name.

CAMELOT

Do you remember old movies with horseback rides through forests, the ones where cathedral-like light traveled from so far above and hit so many branches along the way down that it came on soft and ethereal? This house and all the notions leading to it take me back to those swash-buckling Errol Flynn films that allowed me to travel far beyond my boyhood context. In my real surroundings, the nearest form of mystery and discovery I could find was in the woods and dappled clearings within them. This is one of the gentlest and most dramatic experiences of light—and one that seems almost impossible to re-create.

This house speaks to that boy alone in the woods. It is a fortress, a tree house on the ground, a great and elegant campsite. Staying thin and bright and engaged, it doesn't heap itself on itself as a mansion might. Never more than one room deep, it communes with its surroundings, unleashed from the burden of wondering what anyone might think of it.

As Elizabethan as it is modern, the house dips into a romantic language. There is thunder in it, but also the accompanying sound of velvet. It is hero and heroine, masculinity and femininity, bravery and kindness. These are opposites and great complements. When those massive stone chimneys and the transparent veiling of glass come together, there is rapture. Great bays of windows with literally thousands of panes bring the outside in as if through netting. Although primarily glass, the house doesn't allow anything to come at you too fast. Veiling itself, the light calms you. When you are inside, you are in deep woods and dappled light.

The property itself is a touchstone—the boyhood home of the man who lives there now. When you're in a place that is so like a memory, you know you can bank on your experience and feel safe. Wonderful things have been said and happened to you there. You might have built a campfire in that spot for years and your friends wandered in, but this has evolved from a flame into a glass house. There's an offering in that. It's a great trick to turn a thing in your mind into a thing in this world.

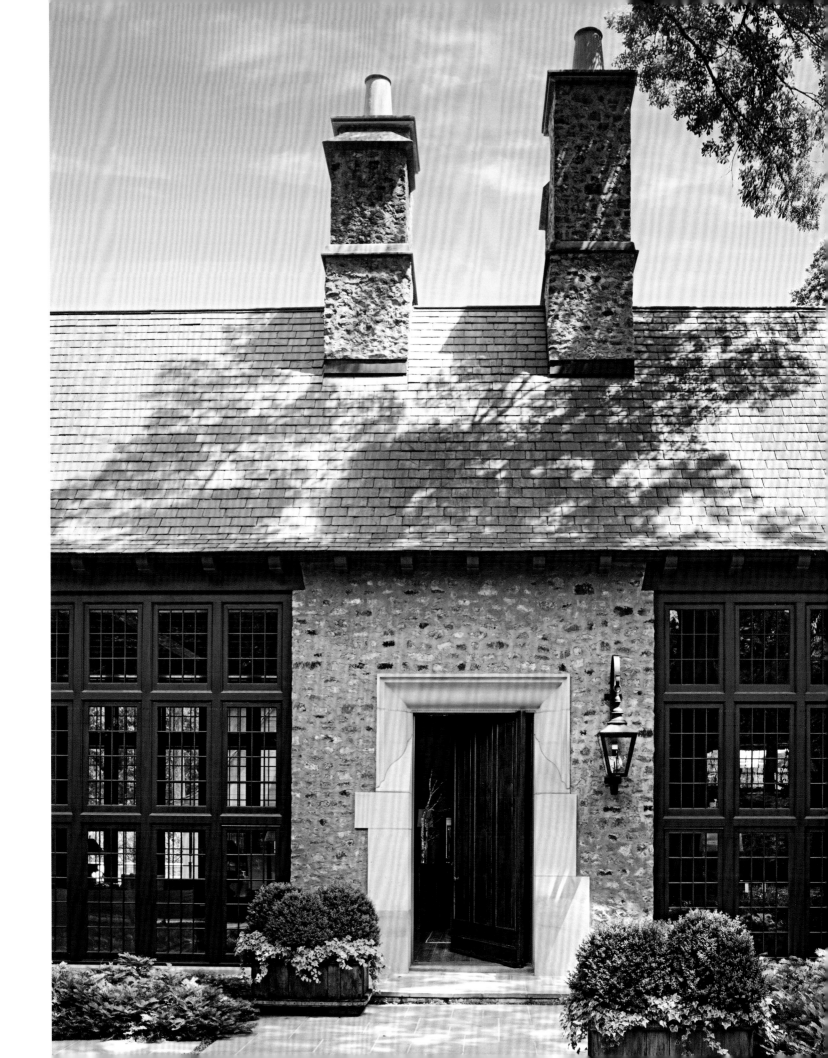

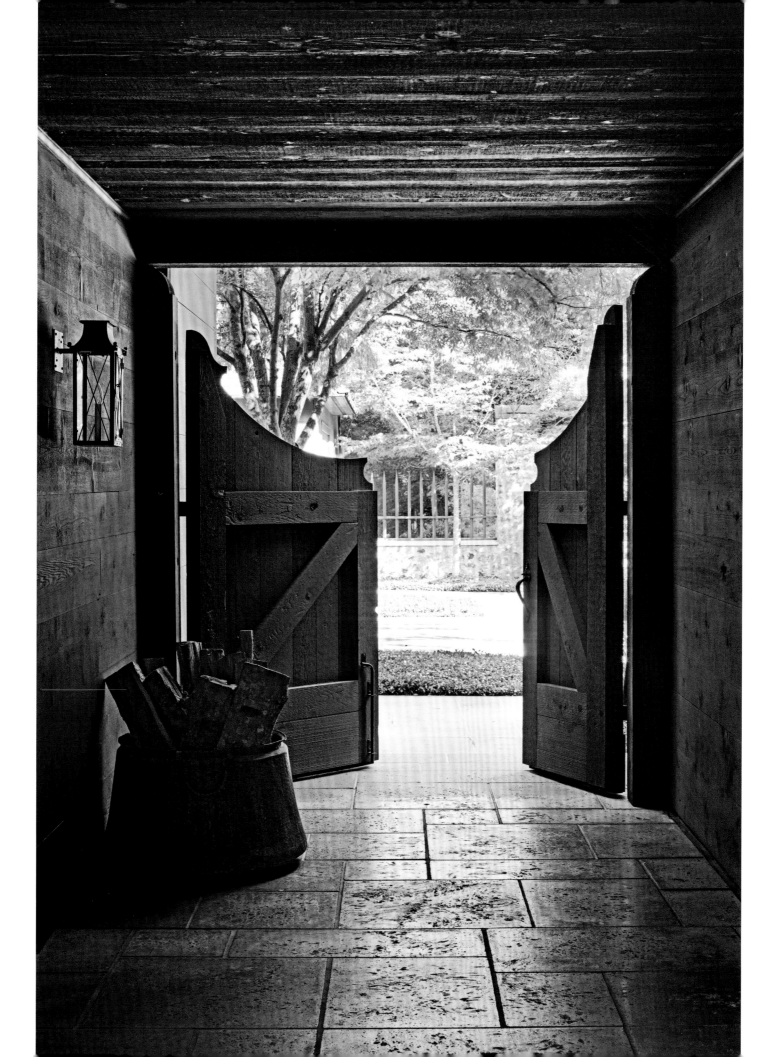

ELATION

The sea belongs to everyone. Anything can show up on a beach or be left at its shore. This is the architectural context of a house on the sea—a limitless invitation that has more to do with who or what washed up than anything familiar. This house comes on strong with an exotic and flavorful character. It is the mysterious personage at the dinner table. Moorish or Egyptian or Russian or French, its roots are difficult to pin down. It is a combination of strengths with little to no timidity in its expression.

In the vastness and bleakness of an ocean setting where everything is large, there seemed no need for this house to conform to a residential language. Instead, it belongs to the scale and drama of a Parisian department store built in the time bridging the Industrial Revolution and the birth of modern style. Being inside is like being locked up overnight in a glamorous store and pretending it's your house. It's a shameless place—and that is part of its wonder. You have the feeling that something almost illegally extravagant is going to happen to you there.

This may be a beach house, but it's one with cast-iron columns, coffered ceilings, and marble floors. It could be a petite palace built in anticipation of the arrival of a great foreign entity that perhaps never showed up— a residence prepared just for that moment, for that brief but exhilarating passage. You can almost imagine how titillated the local artisans would have been, making fine things they were rarely asked to make and employing rare goods that were just too excessive for daily use. Nothing would have been too much for this extraordinary event.

The house's atmosphere is not so much that of a residence as of a great happening or a trip. It provokes an exuberant state of mind—an elation that can't belong to the everyday. It's a high and a dream and as dreams go, borrows freely and sidesteps the ordinary. When you are there, you feel a little bit confounded and terribly attracted. It's a feeling you may not understand but know you want more of. Therein lies the invitation—nothing is too big to think about or dream about or want or imagine. This is the scale of life out of bounds.

VOYAGER

This house is, in Hollywood language, what a man having an affair with the world—a voyager—might build. Far exceeding American standards, it recollects the finest and most moving things he might have seen in Europe. With plaster walls and timbering, leaded windows and restoration glass, slate roofs and a tower, it possesses all the architectural bones you could want for a poetic story. Here, the elements of the grand life—a stair tower, a

two-story bay window, a mezzanine—are distilled into a bouillon cube of a cottage. Simply by changing the scale of these elements, it would be possible to transform this miniature house into a grand manor.

Built by a builder as his own retreat, the house feeds an appetite for integrity and authentic execution. This is not a place of veneers—everything you see is real. Like an English cottage made of rubble from the fields

and timbers cut from trees on the land, it is composed of ingredients that belong to the earth. It is, in a way, built of salt and sugar and flour—not exotic or sophisticated materials, but staples that create a baseline of trust. The rolling, bucolic landscape around it could easily exist in another country and another time—it supports the story completely.

When I think about this house, I think about the side with the big bay window—that great,

gathering eye that looks across the property. As in a lot of English cottages and particularly English chapels, you enter the inner sanctum not through the face, but around the side. This allows you to approach unseen before rediscovering that giant compound eye of a window from a place of security. On the upper floor, there is another viewing place—a glass box of a room that is simultaneously inside and outside. The stair is a scene changer between the two—a gap of silence that allows you a few moments to be alone with yourself. Almost monastic in its quiet, it holds its energy inward. Being there is all about how wondrous it is to be inside a sculpture, knowing that you will be released into that glass room above.

Both miniature and grand, this house has one of everything that ever moved or touched you. It makes you feel simultaneously big and small. As layered and varied as the pages of a book, it offers moments of clarity and context accompanied by introspection and self-study. The thing about a cottage is that it remains forever etched in your heart—it is an emotional sketch drawn with the fewest strokes and most memorable markings. With one of everything and two of nothing, the potency of this house is not redundant. Compacting itself into a star, it holds you always in its architecture. A reduction of everything you know, it is a beautiful place to begin a story and to end it.

LANTERN

To be meaningful and emotionally true, a house needs to be responsive to its context, have a sense of place, and bear witness to what is most important about that place. This was the vision of McAlpine partner Ray Booth and his husband, John, who wanted to set down roots, designing and building their own home in the hills of Nashville. On visiting their chosen site, they discovered foundations of a house that had stood there before—one that had been struck by lightning and burned to the ground. For their house to grow out of this particular place, it needed to spring from the ruins of what had been there before.

Set on a hilltop with sides falling away in every direction, this is very much a tree house in the woods of Tennessee. From its vantage, there is a dramatic view of the city of Nashville—a feature that became the master of every decision. Composed of stone-colored brick, the street facade steps down gently to the earth and the ruins. The front of the house is private in its brick masonry, but around the sides and back it opens into glass. With giant box-bay windows looking down the hill and corners made of glass, it's as if the house exposes its heart and soul to the city below.

Gradual unveiling combined with instances of sudden revelation define the house's rhythm. The front door opens into the side of a giant box-bay window overlooking the woods. Upon entering, you turn to find a passage with a two-story-high ceiling and dark planked walls that act like blinders, focusing your line of sight on the room beyond. This moment of surprise engages you fully with the house upon entry, but a scrim suspended between the hall and living room creates a momentary pause. The intrigue of it pulls you toward the view, but also slows the speed at which it comes on. Your eyes are directly focused on downtown Nashville, but you can't quite see it. Then you step into the main salon and stand right at the edge of the precipice and the view beyond.

Dark-framed and multifaceted, the living room's box-bay window collects images of the city and the surrounding woods and projects them into the interior. The blues of the sky, the light gray and silver of the clouds, and the bluish-purple of the distant mountains became the inspiration for rooms that mirror their surroundings. Like a cabin in the Tennessee hills, the ceilings are planked in gray-brown wood. Dark wood floors have a quieting presence—they don't interrupt what's around them.

All of this grounds the house in a sense of place. A lantern on a hill, it is a lens for witnessing an extraordinary view and a place to call home.

FANTASY

You can leave this world and climb up high enough to see it from an unlimited perspective. That is the message of this stone tower standing in the gardens of a historic Tudor-style house—a place possessing the potential to become a fairyland. One of several buildings added to the gardens, the folly was conceived as a gift from a father to his daughter. Solid as rock, sheer as dreams, it exists somewhere in the realm between reality and fantasy. To demonstrate that this is an achievable realm, one that can be conquered within a lifetime—that is its aim.

At the base, huge boulders emerge from the earth, hinting at the wealth beneath its surface. Chamfered corners blur the edges of the tower's rubble-stone shaft, creating a form that is primitive and rustic. Neither square nor octagonal, its form is nothing we can recognize. At the top, the tower resolves into a precise, discernable shape—a glass box with a 360-degree view. Lofty, unencumbered by any other purpose than your being there, this is a clear and lucid place. Part lookout tower, part sleeping porch, part library—this is where you discover what it means to become elevated. Perhaps that's why books are there—to hasten the journey from reality to romance.

By the time the tower ascends from its very earthen floor to the lovely things at its top, there is an evolution. What is rustic becomes refined. This can happen within the passage of verticality. With no aim other than to lift your heart and elevate your mind, the folly witnesses that life can be anything you want. Such things are possible through architecture, but they can't always be achieved within the more practical vehicles of a new house or a different house. Sometimes what your heart desires might seem foolish, but ultimately it is imperative. Its tangible expression may be the best landmark you can leave behind.

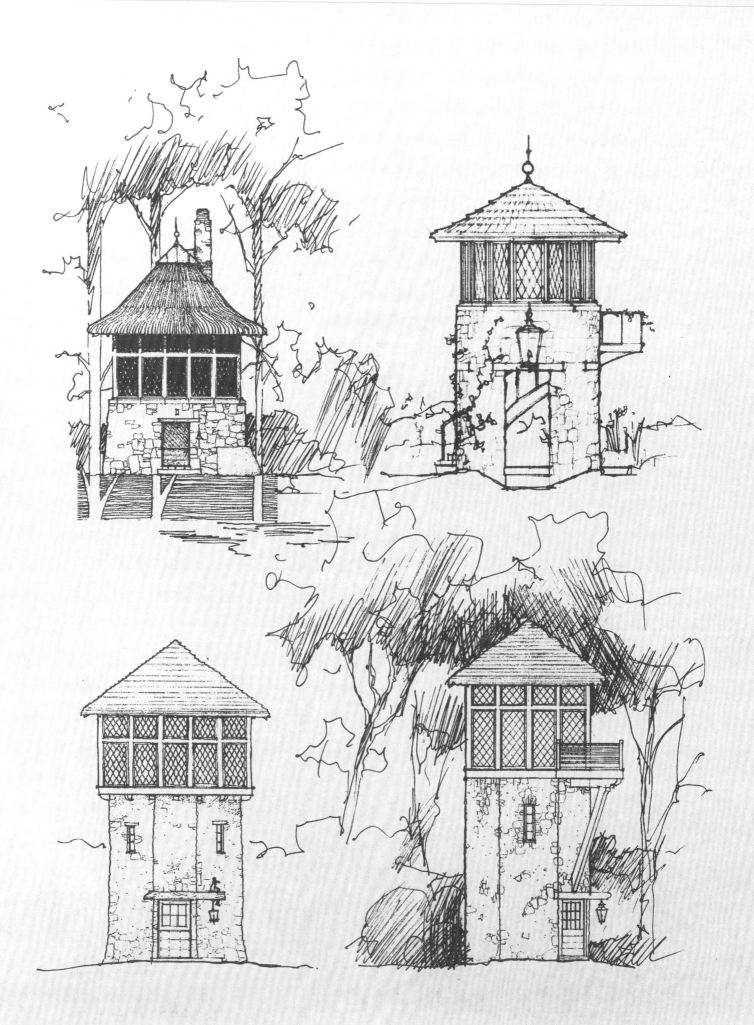

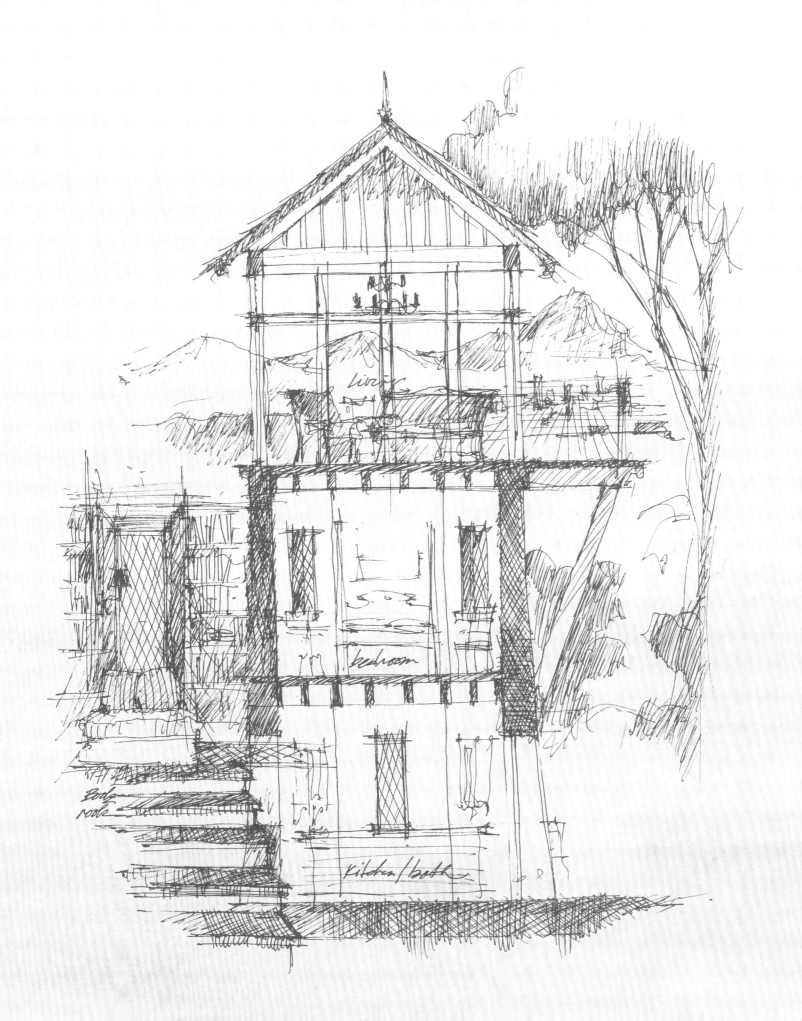

PORTRAIT

Some houses are greater than the sum of their parts. They may be filled with comfortable furniture and colors pleasing to the eye, but that's just a start. They are also portraits of the people who created them—the places they've been, the passions they possess, the things and ideas that intrigue them. They contain objects that have been picked up but never quite put down—things that are constantly moved around the house, finding new partners and engaging in new conversations. A house like this is never static. Its decoration isn't about making things just so—it's about sparking relationships and communication.

Designed by McAlpine partner Susan Ferrier, who lives there with her husband, Adrian, this house is both a portrait of the artist and a bit of a sorceress's cave. It is a place to pull together things in ways that resonate—seductive soft fur rugs, an improbably large antique lantern, geodes, giant shells, a taxidermied swan. It is a laboratory in which to combine elements in various combinations until the right one is found—arrangements that cast spells of earthy magic, engaging the senses in surprising ways. When things come together like this, they give off a kind of effervescence that animates a room.

There is magic in this house, but there is also math—mass, scale, and frequency. If there is one reflective surface in a room, there should be two, creating a rhythm that moves the eye between each flash of reflectivity. The scale of a thing should go as far as it can go, and when you reach the point where you can go no further, you find the opposing gesture. In the master bedroom, a five-foot-tall Italian lantern hangs like a giant stalactite, met by the stalagmite of a tower of bleached-white vintage suitcases. In the dining room, the giant gilt crown of a tester bed, transformed into a chandelier, hangs upside down over a low stone table—all beneath the gaze of a monumental painting of an elephant.

Originally, a goodly portion of the collection was arranged in the library, a cabinet of curiosities with cases of books, glass vitrines containing natural specimens, antique French postal scales, and a nineteenth-century press. A wall-sized map of nineteenth-century London and a chandelier inspired by armillary spheres designed by ancient observers to chart the universe suggest a desire to keep things in their place. But objects in this room have a habit of coming and going and shifting around. It's as though there is a tide moving through, leaving them on shore then taking them away. This is the way of houses that live and breathe.

GATHERING

The first word that comes to mind when you see this house isn't building or place—it's gathering. Spreading out and circling around itself on a drift of land beneath a hill, it issues a silent invitation to come. Diminishing its magnitude by dividing itself into wings and outbuildings, the house makes itself approachable. Although the central facade comes on strong with tall windows and a powerful chimney, the entry remains tiny and modest. Its roof bows down so low you can almost touch it. This is the beginning of a story that isn't sewn up in a single, thunderous note. Instead it trails on with a porte cochere and carriage house, laundry wing and gardening shed—utilitarian buildings that tell the truth and brew the charm of the whole composition. Clearly and honestly expressed, these parts relate the story of a house that might have begun modestly as a family's farm and flourished over the centuries. Together, they express all the elements comprising a full life.

Inspired by the heritage of North Carolina and the pastoral quality of the property, the architecture acquired a rambling kind of classicism. While a colonial list of ingredients with an almost A. Hays Town quality of authenticity is present, the composition is not limited by precedent. From the pigeonnier to the carriage house, every element is correct in detail and proportion, but the recipe of their combining has been changed. In this carefree assembling of white columns and clapboard, stone and slate, there is clamor and celebration, laughter and gregariousness. Although dressed in extraordinarily conservative clothing, it has a very romantic attitude—it's a picnic with powdered wigs.

In houses like these, there is usually a sole place you could imagine making you happy. It's unknown which one of its pieces you will find most endearing. Most likely it will not be the one you expect. You might find joy in the little teahouse-breakfast room pavilion or the breezeway with the swings. Someone else might delight in the gated garden or the pigeonnier. Others might respond to the whole of it, the coming upon the house and its outbuildings assembled beneath the hill like a little colonial army. When you think about the emotional experiences a house can offer, this one is richly coursed. There are so many moments, any one of which could paint a beautiful life.

LUMINOUS

Have you ever seen a place that looks more like home than any other place you've seen? When two world travelers discovered the Dutch Colonial houses of Cape Town, everything in their heart was triggered. In the milk-white walls and fanciful parapets, they found gladness, simplicity, and wholesomeness. There is something that occurs in colonial locales where a style incubated by the home country, executed naively in its colony, takes on a sweetness, a kindness, and an innocence that makes it ever more approachable than the original. The desire for this house was to capture that style and story line and do so with a deep sense of authenticity.

Sitting on a point on the shore of a lake, the house can be seen easily from long distances and all sides. Like a gem, it has complete resolve on all four faces. In the language of Cape Town houses, mock-Baroque parapets add stat-

ure to the gables. Juxtaposed with verticality and order, their curves allow for femininity. From tiny windowpanes the dimension of an open palm to the Vermeer quality of light and texture inside its rooms, the elements of its design are trackable to so many things Dutch. Any one of its chambers is reminiscent of a centuries-old interior. The wall and floor of the entrance hall resemble a Dutch Old Master painting. In a still-life composition, game from the hunt might easily be found hanging beneath the kitchen's mantel.

In part, the house's elegance comes through its simplicity. The great central entrance hall is followed by a dining room and a living room that run the full depth of the house. Both thunderous and quiet in its proportions, the living room is made luminous by windows on three sides. Enormous in scale, the giant oriel win-

dow at one end becomes both room and window. Usually an element projecting from a tower, the oriel floats just above the ground, creating a place to witness the live oak trees and lake. This is where the house breaks form, taking liberties with colonial South African style. There were no places so vulnerable in the originals.

In this country, the house's appearance seems exotic. It is starched and pressed into its setting like a white ruffled collar in a shadowy Dutch Old Master painting. It feels both familiar and far away. Instantly iconic and memorable, it is much less mysterious than it seems. Whether you see it from across the lake, the walled garden, or any place within, it is big and beautiful and easy to understand. Ultimately, it's a house that's just plain pretty. Being there is a fine day—and a romantic one that feeds your heart.

PROSPECT

This is a house that embraces the outdoors loudly and spontaneously. Pressed into a hill on one side and flying out from the ground toward the view on another, it has an enormous range of prospect. From where it sits, the world is large and the sky is huge. With rustic stone walls, an aged tile roof, and very thin steel windows with enormous glass panes, this house in the Maryland hills recalls the architecture of Southern California. Like a Spanish Colonial mission or a ranch, it is essentially one room deep, addressing the property from all sides. This ability to survey a vastness of land from your house is a guiding piece of its Western romance.

The hillside face feels almost like a working farmyard—a place to tie up your horses or come out from the barn to work in the sunlight. In the way barns tend to acquire utilitarian wings and sheds, it has a relaxed asymmetry. The rear is extremely rustic, with doors and windows far larger than a house of this height would have. Enormous openings wide enough for a wagon or tractor to pass through possess the agricultural scale and language of a very grand barn or a Napa Valley winery. The oversized shutters might have been barn doors before the building was given glass. These soften the scale of the doors and windows, but mostly they are there as reminders that once upon a time this building might have been something else.

This is a house where the ancient and modern meet. It is extremely rustic, but it also has liberal interior space and large apertures—a combination that rarely exists in residential language. Sometimes I shift to industrial or agricultural language to achieve this, because those buildings have lofty interiors and massive openings for the passage of equipment. Tapping that architecture solves the riddle more readily than modifying a residential model.

Therein lies the casual nature of this house and also its power. It is strong but not pretentious. It is at once important and informal. It seems only recently to have been used as a house, and that gives it resonance and strength. This unlikely pairing creates generous volumes, bright, clear light, and far-reaching transparency. When you look at the front of the house, you can almost imagine driving a wagon piled high with hay right through the wide opening into the arena of the house. There's something Western in that. Free of convention or any primness, this house has the broad-stroke thinking of a maverick rancher.

INTRIGUE

Poised on hilly terrain, this house hangs above a shimmering Southern metropolis as if overlooking a harbor of lights. By the time you travel from the entrance to the grand salon at its rear, you are standing several floors above ground and hundreds of feet above the city. Blown out with windows on the back, the house required opaqueness on the street side to make it feel less vulnerable. Nearly blank except for a classical pediment, the facade appears to belong not so much to a house as to a little embassy representing a country you could never quite remember the name of. There is a clue missing—and this becomes a platform for the house's intrigue.

Behind this opaque facade lies an entrance gallery with an enormous scrim that allows you to see what lies beyond only in silhouette. Very much a device from the language of theatre, the gauzy wall brings things into focus slowly. You have to walk around it to see the salon clearly and discover the city it floats above. This buys a little time, allowing you to be greeted, received into the house, and prepared for the incredible view.

The interior has the evolved elegance of a Parisian apartment. With moldings and profiles in very low relief, everything comes on softly with a quiet voice. Accompanying this subtlety of detail are stature and dignity, rhythm and a whispered reverence. There is a Gustavian *blanc*-ness—the hush of an elegant house shut down for the season. When you look at the living room, you can almost imagine it draped with sheets.

Galleries, long rooms, and threaded axes invite linear progression through the house. They become walking sequences long enough to allow you to complete a thought, to walk the house meditatively in an almost monastic way. There is a certain *Om* experience present the moment you enter—a gap of silence. Prayerful, a little reverent, quiet, dressy, and exciting, the house has its own odd set of adjectives.

TRUST

This is a house that's comfortable with itself. It's so solid and relaxed that you feel safe when you are there. You get the same feeling around certain people who emit trust and evoke it because there is something so natural in their integrity. When people know who they are and are honest about it, they create a sense of security. Architecture can do the same thing. When a house remains for the most part one room deep, it becomes transparent. Even if its composition appears casual or disheveled, its order and intelligence are evident. There is vulnerability in its transparency and reassurance in its order.

There's a certain humility about the way this house lies on the land. It doesn't stand on a pedestal. Instead, it rests below a hill, pressing slightly into the ground. You have to look down to see it. With an entry facade shaped like an L, it stretches out an arm to capture you and pull you in. Because it sits lower than the street, the house lifts up its head to greet you with tall gables and a steep roof. I always think of houses and dogs as having similar postures—a really good dog will hold itself low to the ground but lift its head to let you know it's safe to approach. That alternating rhythm of modesty and statuesque verticality is a characteristic I love.

A sleepier language exists at the rear of the house, where round, fat columns hold up low, drifting roofs. There is something disarming in the wandering composition of wings and porches and outbuildings. Because you can see straight through the windows to the other side of the house, you always know where you are. Materially, the architecture is very simple. Its elegance is achieved through loose material—irregular quoining and rubble stone that is as nubby as a well-worn sweater. It's a beautiful pairing of kindness and strength.

Sometimes the character of a house is forthright and classical in nature. It knows a thing about itself and wants to make sure you don't miss it. Real, resonant, and relaxed in itself, this is not that kind of house. Like the people who live there, it is quietly composed and compassionate. Like a shepherd's cottage, it's a place where you feel welcome and safe. You drift into it easily and know you can depend on it.

VESSEL

Moored between a boardwalk and the ocean like a ship come to shore, this house captures the romance of the sea. There is a feeling that a ship's captain might once have lived there, or a watchman. Rising like a half-moon between steep gables, the barrel-shaped roof is something a shipbuilder might have imagined. Spanning the house from side to side and end to end, the roof has the explosive energy of a sail filled with wind. With shutters like hatches and porches like prows, it tells a story of voyage and adventure and of returning home.

The great gathering space inside is raised high above the dunes. From it, you can look down on the waves and feel as though they are lifting you up. There is a ravaged, weathered aspect to its walls of pecky cypress that look as though winds and sands have blown across them, leaving their mark. The ceiling is so lofty and the window so large you feel suspended between water and sky. Here, the ocean is the theatre and the dining room's long altar table is the stage. It is a call to dinner at the captain's table—a gesture of magnitude and of reverence to the host, which is the sea.

The whole house is a wooden vessel. If it were a Hollywood set for an old seafaring movie, everything would be colored in shades of pewter and brown. In the nautical allusions it makes, the architecture should be sepia in tone, but it has been brightened. It's like a 1930s black-and-white film faded almost to white from exposure to light and the passing years. This makes it a more light-hearted story. There is pleasure and optimism in it. A ship has a lot to do with the capacity to transport. This one lifts the spirit, altering gravity and taking all the heaviness away.

ADVENTURE

Things have traveled a long way to get to this house—masks from Africa, baskets woven in Panama, ebonized tusks from France, Baroque chairs from Italy. But this is not a story about travel and acquisition. It's one about having adventure on the planet and coming home again, of voyaging into the unknown without untying the strings that hold us to earth. Being here is not exactly "glamping," but there is a quality of exploring the world from a sophisticated perspective.

This is the most glamorous safari tent you can ever imagine. The walls are hung with velvet and damask, and plush carpets cover the floor. With a base of hinged iron that looks as though it could fold flat, the living room's coffee table might be an extravagantly heavy piece of campaign furniture. Smaller in stature and more easily disassembled, two carved Italian Baroque hall chairs could fit into a traveling trunk. The room's mural of silhouetted trees might be the view seen through the flap of a tent and the huge map of London with heavily creased folds, something an explorer would carry as a memento of the place he left and to which he will return.

The house is heavily influenced by the travels of two people and their fascination with cultures very different from their own. The artifacts in its room are not just souvenirs—they reflect a world view. This was an opportunity to introduce something primitive into an ethereal environment, because both reside within our nature. All the rooms have a limited palette, with silk, fur, and reflective surfaces giving a sense of depth. Furnishings of stone, wood, and metal represent the elements and the sensual, earthy nature of their adventures.

This is an Italianate villa, all math and symmetry, filled with African fertility figures and wooden masks decorated with shells and animal hair. The house's large spaces are an invitation for large gestures, like the long French industrial table in the living room and the larger-than-life painting of a bare man's back visible from the entrance hall. Just because something is raw and elemental doesn't mean it isn't also sophisticated and in good taste. For all the luxury and refinement in this house, there is always something naked and honest that grounds you. Being here is like taking your hand and wiping it across a surface of shiny pebbles to reveal the earth lying beneath.

RECOLLECTION

Whether it transpires within the territory of the heart or an actual returning to a place, there is something powerful about remembering where you're from. Going back to a place you know and reshaping it into something more than you can remember—perhaps even more than it ever was—feeds the child in you. When one man regathered the pieces of a tract of land known to him and his father and his grandfather and reassembled them into a single property, it was a curative act. Putting up a historic decommissioned fire tower, he cast a nurturing eye over the memories he had recovered and reforested 250 acres of longleaf pine. Without his stewardship, this land would have been empty terrain with no one to tend it or care about its fate.

When he first reclaimed this wilderness in the middle of nowhere in Alabama, there was no place to be. Essentially, the eye of it had to be invented—an invitational place that was verdant and cool with a humble cabin sipping at the edge of a lake. Sitting right in the shallows, the cabin offers the experience you so rarely get, when the water and the architecture meet. A little shed down by the fishing hole for boats and paddles and the gear of fishing and the tying of flies was all else that was needed.

This is a woodsman's spiritual retreat, so everything in its language needed to be dressed that way, with exposed rafter tails and rough wood siding. Painted the colors you wear in the woods, the cabin is red flannel long johns and the fishing shed, olive-colored hunting clothes. Here, you know you can come as you are. With all its shagginess and grasses, even the landscape supports the story of being beautifully unkempt. This is the kind of place you find—rarely the kind you build.

To fish from your porch or shoot from your window is a crazy idea—it's something a king might think of. There are a million reasons not to do it, but in this case, it was necessary. There's something purifying about removing everything between you and the water so there isn't even land anymore. It's just you in a safe place at the edge. Those box seats and the chance to kiss the brim of the water is all the evidence of grace we need before we turn back around and continue our lives.

RESONANCE

When a pair of designer industrialists set roots in Napa Valley on a hillside above the Silverado Trail, they were unable to find anything in the surrounding architecture that matched what Napa looked like in their hearts. The most appropriate structures they could find were the winery buildings. Their mission was to build something that felt as if it belonged to the place, that looked indigenous and not an import from Tuscany or Spain. Let's forget what's here and crack the code of what should be. Let's write the DNA of an architecture that never really existed and create an aesthetic that looks like Napa feels.

With local stone, steel windows, and a concrete shingle roof reflecting the distant gray of hilltops, the house blends into its surroundings. Exactly the color of the atmosphere, with a little mascara added by the steel windows, it is an expressive thing that does not interfere with its natural context. Low-slung on top of a ridge, it's invisible from the Silverado Trail but still captures light and wide-ranging views of the landscape. The premise was that the house should ramble and remain one room deep wherever you are, affording maximum occasion for witnessing the land and tapping into its healing properties. Rolled into this relaxed posture is a tremendous amount of sequencing and unfolding, drama and romance.

The house doesn't come on obviously. Wandering and wrapping around itself, it creates as many outdoor rooms as inside spaces, blurring the distinction between the two. Entering from around and to one side, you arrive at a loggia of stone pillars and rugged oak beams illuminated by a crystal chandelier. A necessary contradiction, this is the Western grit and European appetite that is Napa. Clothed in elegance but delivered to the surrounding land by walls of glass, the grand salon is as worldly as it is down-to-earth. An extremely gregarious kitchen can handle a hillside of people helping and serving, and the kitchen lounge is terribly comfortable for just two or three. This house is intimate, but it has qualities that make you feel grand. There is magnitude in its apertures and vast views. You are always walking toward lofty elements. This is an emotional landscape that holds you and transports you, and the house mirrors that. Wrapping you in its arms, it shows you the surrounding bounty.

STORYBOOK

Houses in the English style, expressed in miniature, dot the streets of Mountain Brook Village, a 1920s neighborhood outside Birmingham. As diminutive as it is ultimately dramatic, this house shows up in that context as a friendly presence. Despite the many rooms and courtyards behind it, the street facade has the wide-eyed, humble features of a furry creature. In my heart, I wanted this to be a kindly Br'er Rabbit of a house, with the ingredients of its demeanor—knobby stone, timbering, and light symmetry. Multifaceted leaded windows with restoration glass tilt the whole composition even further toward a storybook existence.

This is a very un-American house in that it doesn't throw all its wares to the street or peak in the first act. In a trait of many English houses, it is wholly symmetrical on the garden side, but not on the front. Its grandeur is deferred to the last, when you turn around and realize what a strong and balanced place you're in. There is drama and pomp and circumstance in the way the wings and courtyards progress behind the house. Gradually, they unfold toward a tiny stone structure at the back of the garden that stands on a raised green surrounded by woods. This could easily be the hermitage of an English country estate—there is that much feeling of sanctuary and romance.

The house itself is very much like a little timbered theatre—a perfect set for a Victorian farce or Agatha Christie's *The Mousetrap*. With mezzanines overlooking all three sides of the living room, it's possible to interact with the upper and lower floors diagonally from any place you stand. You can address every room or speak to anyone from its center, and anyone can open a door, lean over the rail, and answer. Matching staircases hide behind the living room's fireplaces. Although they are symmetrically opposed, one fireplace is heightened in its expression and the other, lessened. Within the tit-for-tat symmetry of the house, there is also an off-kilter energy that softens the balance. Imagine a symmetrical face with two eyes and one of them is winking—the imperfection makes you want to love it.

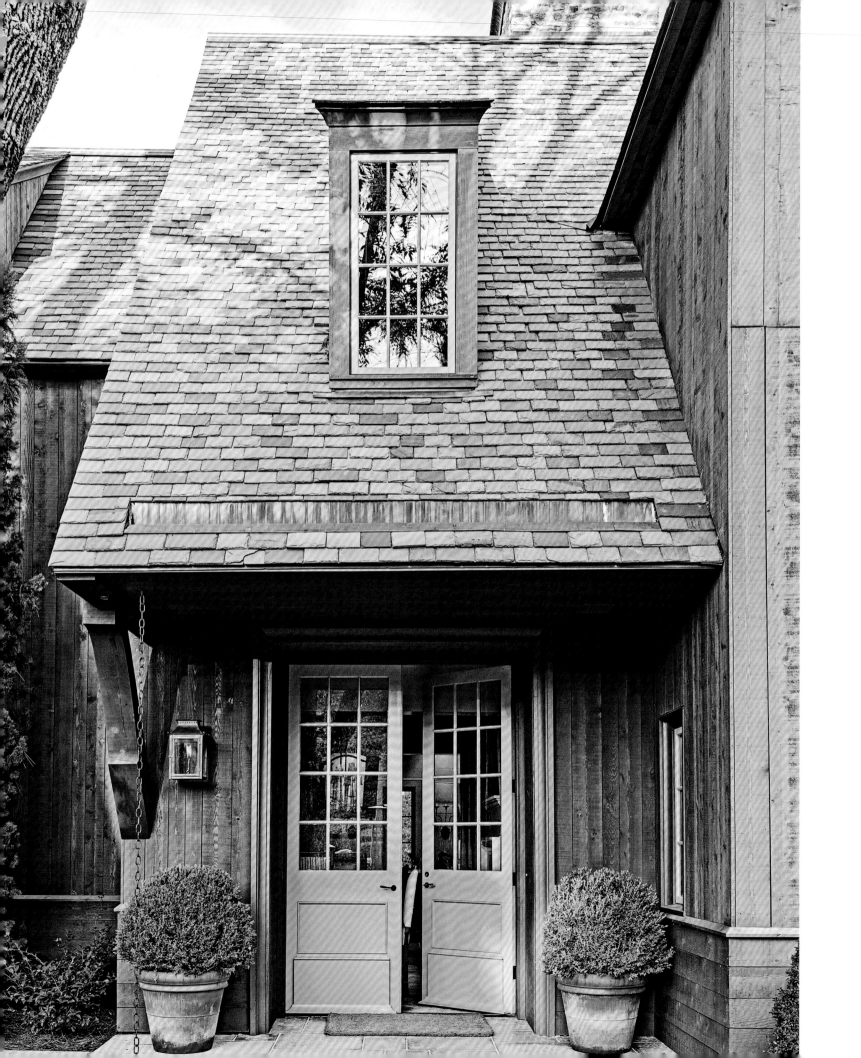

WELCOME

This house is shaped like a perfect piece of pie. Overlooking a quaint intersection where five streets come together, it has two street fronts and three faces. From the sidewalk, you can see almost every part and piece of it and read the floor plan by looking at its windows. It has no secrets because there's nothing to hide. Positioned in what is, in a way, the mayoral seat of the neighborhood, it has a certain responsibility. Surrounded by wood-frame houses expressed in Colonial American style, it is ringed by suburbs predominantly English in sensibility. Recognizably American, but with English roots, this house bridges the two.

The steep gables are a take on Carpenter Gothic churches, and the plank siding is something you'd find in an American barn, but the low-rolling slate roof is a breakaway that harks back to the English.

The house is a tad exotic, but it's also familiar. It has a carpenter's approachability that is sewn up in cotton thread. Asymmetrical shutters swinging this way and that give the gables the unconcerned expression of a barn that doesn't know you're looking at it. Because there is no ceremonial front to the house, there is no grand entrance. Tucked away on one side beneath a sheltering eave, the entry offers a back-door, come-as-you-are invitation.

Inside this house, you find everything you imagined about it to be true. The main living area unfolds into two ample rooms. Gregarious and openhearted, the dining room comes on fast. A double-sided fireplace follows—the only division between the dining room and a family room with walls of mullioned windows. This house is as clear and forthright as a good friend. It's an everyday kind of place that fits a small family or a crowd of neighbors. Warm with big pockets, it's like a favorite winter coat you can't wait to get back into. It will take care of you.

RAMBLE

This is not an emblematic house. It is a place of comfort and shade. Textured and casual, it's glad to see you and glad to see everything beyond it. A 1940s weekend-in-the-country, woody-wagon kind of house, it rambles around a rolling hillside. I wasn't asked for an American Colonial or New England–style house, but the wholesome primness of that was such a good setup for the rest of the story. Upright and proper on the entry face, the house relaxes at the rear with naive columns like fat milk bottles that hold up long, lilting roofs. There is innocence in those plump columns and eaves pulled down low like the brim of a hat that plays to the Saturday that is this house.

There is also an element of comedy in the house. It is a bit like Claudette Colbert, the great comedic actress who could be elegant and a little daffy at the same time. That's what makes it so good to be around. Buttoned-up on the entry face, it lets its seams out at the back. The roof is steep on the front, but it settles down slowly behind. It has no trumpeting voice. The loudest noise it would make is the flap of a sheet in the wind. Beneath it, big-eyed windows look out with an expression of gladness.

There was no obvious sense of place about this site, so the house had to spread out and curl around itself to create one.

Porches wrap the rear and wings and outbuildings amble in front. The feeling is of someone having a picnic, unfurling a cloth to create a place for the happening to come. Or of a woman with a giant skirt who sits down and spreads it out around herself. In that, there is an invitation to relax.

Sometimes in a relationship, someone is brave enough to say, "I am so happy." Do you remember someone saying that to you and how knowing they were happy made you feel safe and happy, too? This house has kinship with that sentiment. Ultimately, it is a little quiet and a little hushed and terribly generous with itself and its company.

RETREAT

This is a house made for a lumberman—a man whose daily life is in the industry of building. He had acquired a lakefront peninsula lot with a tremendously long and three-dimensional waterfront, and he wanted a house built entirely of wood. Today there are so many available choices of material for every surface in a house. In the land of lumber, wood is the answer to every question—every riddle is solved by wood. All the surfaces in this house are made of wood—edge-grained heart-pine floorboards, rough pine beams, thinly glazed plank sheathing, pine telephone poles. It is a simple interior referencing a time when plaster was too expensive and too exotic for a lakeside house. In today's language, it's exotic to look this humble.

The house is derivative of many things that are not quite a house. Its long chains of windows resemble a fish camp, which to some seems like a sketchy thing built of spare parts. To me as a child, those long chains of windows in lakefront catfish restaurants were glamorous—they had a kind of homemade modernism. Parts of the house with windows shaded by long awnings feel almost like a railroad depot. Back in the days when schools were beautiful, when walls of windows were the only way to light their rooms—that was also a trigger for this house.

This is a place that tips its hat to romance in a variety of unlikely ways. It's definitely more male than female. It's meant to be a gathering place—a comfortable, casual outpost where you take a back seat to the magnificence of the lake. This is what men build when women aren't watching. They put a pole in the living room and don't have to talk anyone into it. There's not a lot of urbanism here. The only imported piece is the Tudor arch appearing in the front entry and one or two places inside. This makes the house feel as though perhaps it was once a woodland church retreat—a place of honesty and healing. It's the truth, the whole truth, and nothing but the truth.

ASCENSION

As primitive as it is unimaginably futuristic, James's Well is a kind of emotional time machine. When you enter it, you are stepping into the stream of a powerful, magnetic duality that exists between heaven and earth. When the parents of a son who died during African missionary work came to me, they were looking for some way to bear witness to his life. They wanted something to capture and convey its meaning and emotion, but they didn't know what that would look like. How do you build something inspired by someone or something you've lost? The answer is you don't build an object, you build an experience.

Asking me to do this was a leap of faith on their part—and it was met with a spontaneous solution. When I stood by James's grave, marked by a pair of logs bound by rope in a cruciform shape, and looked at a little glen across a pond, the entire idea came to me in an instant. We should build a primitive structure formed of rubble—almost of mud—rising to a three-tiered thatched cone roof ending in a glass cube. The small tower would be shaped in plan like a Coptic cross—a form familiar to us as a shape but not as an enterable space. "Vessel" was the word that came to mind to describe the space within. Later I learned that the Coptic cross tracks its origins to Africa. By providence it was exactly right.

Turning a latch at the level of the breastbone—from your heart to James's—you open a twenty-seven-inch plank of African wood to enter the tower. This number recurs in many places within the tower, recording James's final age in dimensions. Inside there is a twenty-seven-inch aperture in the floor, opening to a reservoir of water far larger than you can perceive. Exposing just a portion of the subterranean bounty, its implication is one of plenty. Straight overhead, there is a twenty-seven-inch cube of glass surrounded by sky. Suspended between the well and the cube, a clear and luminous cross hangs—arising, ushering.

Through the isolation of its setting and the intimacy of its space, James's Well is meant to be experienced by one person at a time—to be a solitary passage. There is a powerful kinesis existing within its stillness. A spiritual accelerator, James's Well guides you into a divine connection faster than a more complex environment. The beam that exists between the light above and the water below with the cross in suspension is life itself. That such an elegant and transporting experience can be had within such a crude and primitive structure is a revelation.

Only from the heart can you touch the sky. —Rumi, 1207–1273

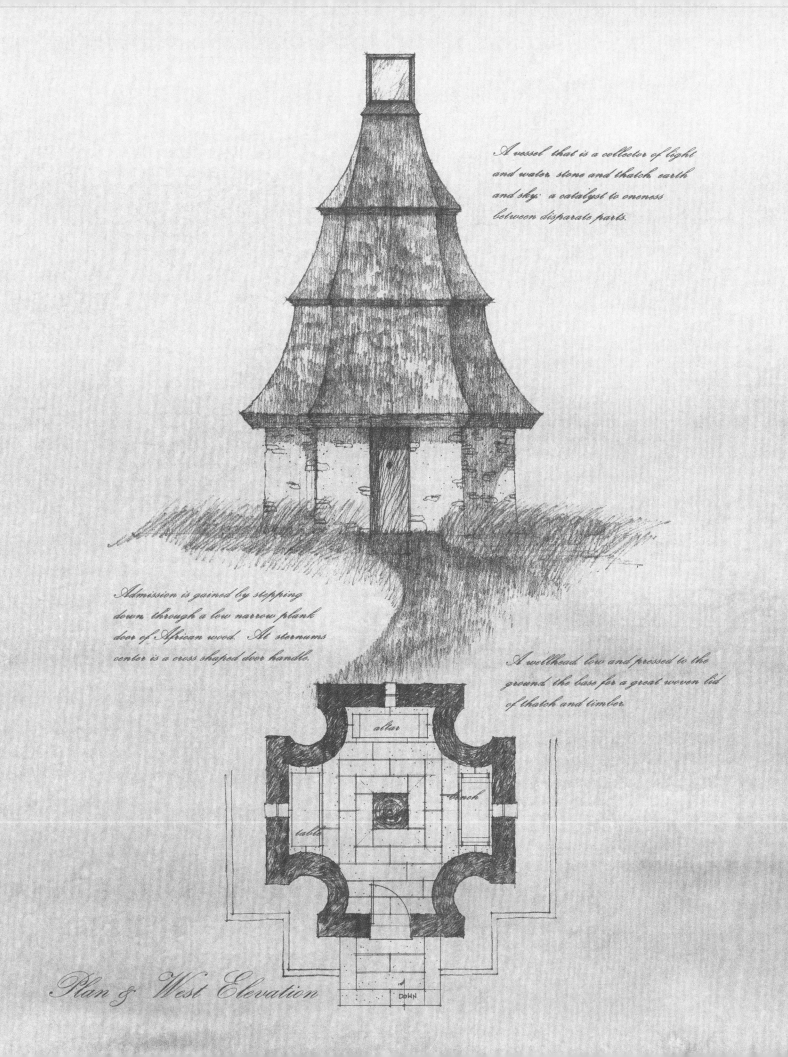

A vessel that is a collector of light
and water, stone and thatch, earth
and sky: a catalyst to oneness
between disparate parts.

Admission is gained by stepping
down through a low narrow plank
door of African wood. At sternums
center is a cross shaped door handle.

A wellhead low and pressed to the
ground the base for a great woven lid
of thatch and timber.

altar

table

bench

DOWN

Plan & West Elevation

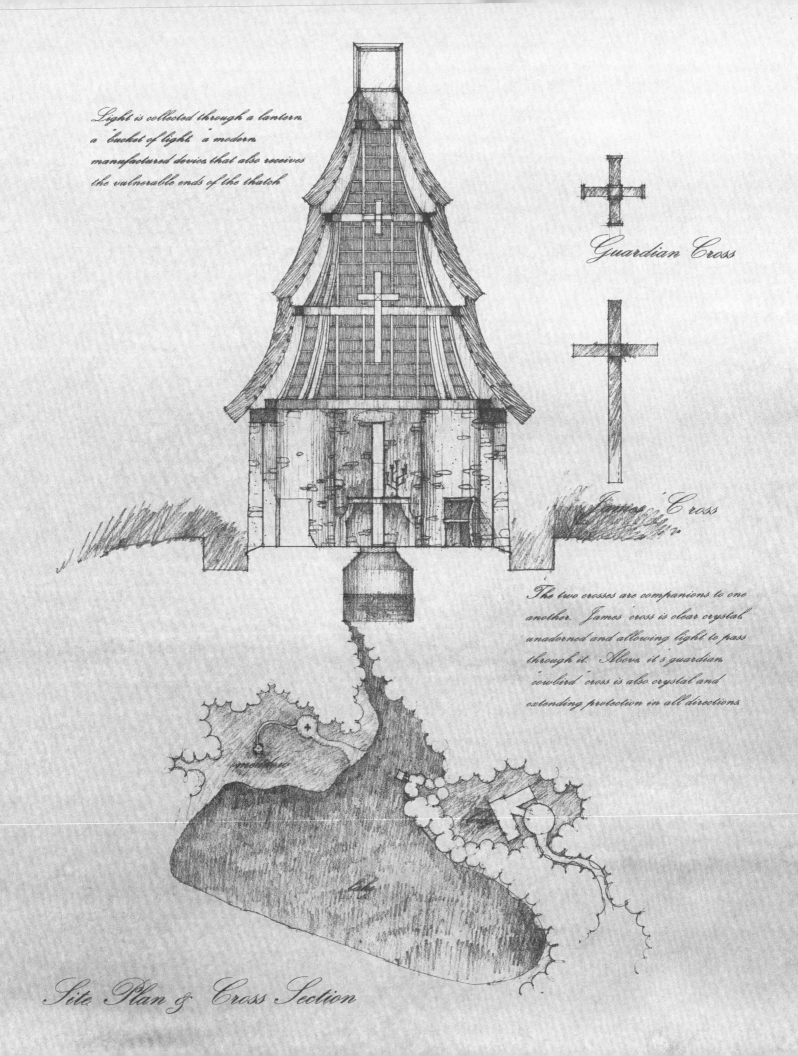

Light is collected through a lantern.
a "bucket of light" a modern
manufactured device that also receives
the vulnerable ends of the thatch

Guardian Cross

James' Cross

The two crosses are companions to one
another. James' cross is clear crystal
unadorned and allowing light to pass
through it. Above it's guardian
"cowbird" cross is also crystal and
extending protection in all directions

Site Plan & Cross Section

CAMELOT, Page 12
ARCHITECTURE
Bobby McAlpine and
Chris Tippett
INTERIOR DESIGN Ray Booth
LANDSCAPE ARCHITECTURE
Mike Kaiser, Kaiser Trabue
Landscape Architecture

Pages 18–19
Relaxed in form, the facade's cut-stone entry is
approachable rather than grand. Immense walls of
windows also offer a welcoming expression.

Pages 20–25
Marrying earthy parged-stone walls with worldly goods
like antique carved-wood angels and a Rococo-style
chandelier, the house speaks a language of its own.
Voluminous velvet drapery divides the rooms.

ELATION, Page 32
ARCHITECTURE
Bobby McAlpine and
Greg Tankersley
INTERIOR DESIGN
Susan Ferrier

Pages 34–37
Glamour and sensuality reign in a salon with lavish
furnishings and a palette of silver, gold, blue, and cream.

Pages 38–39
The exotic shape of the arches hints at both Moorish
and Egyptian influences.

Pages 42–43
Elegant Parisian department stores inspired the
interior's coffered ceilings, marble floors, and the
decorative iron railings of a dramatic stair.

FANTASY, Page 82
ARCHITECTURE
Greg Tankersley
LANDSCAPE ARCHITECTURE
Mike Kaiser, Kaiser Trabue
Landscape Architecture

Pages 82 and 84–85
From a sky-blue door dwarfed by a rubble-stone tower to
the observatory and roof of steam-bent cedar shingles
at the top, this folly has a quaint, storybook appearance.
In the tower's shadowy interior, a staircase climbs to a
luminous glass room that offers a 360-degree view of the
garden and distant mountains.

PORTRAIT, Page 86
INTERIOR DESIGN
Susan Ferrier

Pages 88–91
Treasures in the living room include geodes and shells
arranged on column sections and an antique garden statue
of Hercules. In the dining room, chain-mail drapery
hangs behind a snake-handled urn discovered in Paris.

Pages 100–103
Chenille bed-hangings, a gilded architectural ornament
made into a headboard, an eighteenth-century Italian
lantern, and bleached travel valises compose intriguing
tableaux in the bedroom.

VOYAGER, Page 50

ARCHITECTURE
Bobby McAlpine and
Greg Tankersley

INTERIOR DESIGN
Ray Booth

LANDSCAPE ARCHITECTURE
Ben Page, Page Duke
Landscape Architects

Pages 54–55
Timbering, a slate roof, and bays of leaded-glass windows
lend this house in Alabama the appearance of a European
manor. An immense three-story-tall box-bay window brings
light and views of the bucolic setting into the interior.

Pages 60–61
With polished plaster walls and serpentine forged-iron
railings, the stair tower is sculptural and mysterious.

LANTERN, Page 66

**ARCHITECTURAL AND INTERIOR
DESIGN** Ray Booth

LANDSCAPE ARCHITECTURE
Mike Kaiser, Kaiser Trabue
Landscape Architecture

Pages 72–73
Open railings and two-story windows transform this
residence into a tree house with a view of woods in the
foreground and the city of Nashville, Tennessee, far below.

Pages 76–79
In the dining room and lounge, shades of purple
inspired by the color of distant mountains establish a
peaceful, modern aesthetic.

GATHERING, Page 104

ARCHITECTURE
Bobby McAlpine and
Scott Torode

Pages 108–109
With a symmetrical fieldstone facade, slate roof,
and clapboard wings, this house conforms to traditional
American style.

Pages 112–113
Passing through a picket gate into a boxwood garden, a
stone path leads to the pool terrace and neoclassical pool
house beyond. The charm and intimacy of this progression
balance the architecture's more formal attributes.

LUMINOUS, Page 114

ARCHITECTURE
Bobby McAlpine and
David Baker

INTERIOR DESIGN
Ray Booth

LANDSCAPE ARCHITECTURE
Mike Kaiser, Kaiser Trabue
Landscape Architecture

Pages 120–121
In the hall, wood paneling and muted gray marble
recall the light of a Vermeer painting. The screen between
the front room and hall is based on a historic South
African *porte de vista*.

Pages 122–123
A spacious salon accommodates three gathering areas,
including an intimate alcove inside the ogee window.
This apse-like room appears almost to float on the
surrounding lake.

PROSPECT, Page 136

ARCHITECTURE
Bobby McAlpine and
Chris Tippett

LANDSCAPE ARCHITECTURE
Mike Kaiser, Kaiser Trabue
Landscape Architecture

Pages 136 and 138–139
With red tile roofs, stucco walls, and windows in an
industrial scale, this compound combines Mediterranean
Revival and modern styles. The giant windows open to
embrace a sweeping view of the surrounding landscape.

Pages 140–143
Details like the entryway's Roman arch and a colonnade
with Tuscan columns lend romance to the rugged parged-
stone structure.

INTRIGUE, Page 150

ARCHITECTURE
Bobby McAlpine and
John Sease

INTERIOR DESIGNER
Betsy Brown, Betsy Brown Inc.

LANDSCAPE ARCHITECTURE
Ben Page, Page Duke
Landscape Architects

Pages 154–157
Decorated by interior designer Betsy Brown, the living room
expresses the same hushed elegance as the surrounding
architecture. Sheer blinds filter the light that floods in through
tall windows.

Pages 160–161
With charcoal-brown walls and a gilded chandelier, the dining
room has a dusky glamour that contrasts with the living
room's pearly light. A dining alcove behind an onyx-colored
curtain is a seductively intimate space.

ADVENTURE, Page 194

INTERIOR DESIGN
Susan Ferrier

ARCHITECTURE
Mack McKinney

Pages 196–197
The living room's lush carpeting, drapery, and upholstery
set off the rough texture of African artifacts of metal and
stone and a contemporary stone-topped table.

Pages 198–199
In the dining room, a more feminine aesthetic prevails with
diaphanous curtains, antique botanical prints, and a faux-bois
and jade mirror frame. An antique wrought-iron bracket and
lantern take the place of a traditional chandelier.

RECOLLECTION, Page 202

ARCHITECTURE
Bobby McAlpine and
Lida Cunningham Sease

LANDSCAPE ARCHITECTURE
Guy Williams, DCA Landscape
Architects

Pages 206–209
The architecture of this rural cabin and fishing shed dresses
itself down in order to instill a sensation of comfort and
relaxation. Rough pine board-and-batten walls, exposed rafter
tails, and roofs of shingle and tin are inspired by the simple,
unpretentious architecture of Southern lake camps.

TRUST, Page 170
ARCHITECTURE
Bobby McAlpine and
Chris Tippett
LANDSCAPE ARCHITECTURE
Mike Kaiser, Kaiser Trabue
Landscape Architecture

Pages 171–175
Asymmetrical wings extending from the central bay offer an anthropomorphic gesture of embrace. Large windows aligned from front to back render the house transparent, endowing it with qualities of openness and honesty.

Pages 180–183
Warm-toned, tactile materials, including slathered-stone walls, local Pennsylvania stone, and white oak paneling, are used throughout the interior.

VESSEL, Page 184
ARCHITECTURE
Bobby McAlpine and
David Baker
INTERIOR DESIGN
Susan Ferrier

Pages 188–189
The irregular boards on the underside of an otherwise refined spiral stair resemble something a ship's carpenter might have fashioned. Pecky cypress walls have the tone and texture of sea-weathered wood.

Pages 190–191
The dining room opens up to the upper floor, borrowing light from its windows. Furnishings mirror the colors of sea and sand visible from the balcony outside French doors.

RESONANCE, Page 212
ARCHITECTURE
Bobby McAlpine and
John Sease, with Rela Gleason
INTERIOR DESIGN
Rela Gleason, Rela Gleason
Design

Pages 214–215
Even when its lower panels are closed, tall Dutch doors allow the warm glow of a crystal chandelier to gleam through transom windows at night. Folding shutters on either side can provide privacy to the courtyard beyond or reveal the surrounding landscape.

Pages 216–217
Overlooking a vast view on one side and an intimate courtyard on the other, floor-to-ceiling glass doors and windows make the living room luminous and transparent.

Pages 218–219
Surrounded by sheer walls of glass, a stacked stone fireplace offers a place of warmth and intimacy in the lounge beside the kitchen.

STORYBOOK, Page 224
ARCHITECTURE
Bobby McAlpine and
Scott Torode
INTERIOR DESIGN
Susan Ferrier
LANDSCAPE ARCHITECTURE
Nimrod Long, Nimrod Long
and Associates

Page 225
A cozy entrance is appointed with a fanciful chair and a small fireplace tucked like a mouse hole beneath the low console table. The entrance hall's diminutive scale contrasts with the immense gregariousness of the living space beyond.

Pages 236–237
At the rear, the house wraps itself around a series of courtyards with symmetrical outbuildings that create a sheltered and tranquil cloister.

WELCOME, Page 238

ARCHITECTURE
Bobby McAlpine and
Chris Tippett

INTERIOR DESIGN
Susan Ferrier

LANDSCAPE DESIGN
Landscape Services, Inc.

Pages 242–243
A broad chimneypiece flanked by recessed mirrors separates
the dining room from the family room on the far side.

Pages 244–245
A giant Baroque-inspired mirror and tall Corinthian-column
lamps visually reduce the living room's lofty scale. Muted
shades of green and blue unite the interior with the garden
framed by walls of windows.

RAMBLE, Page 248

ARCHITECTURE
Bobby McAlpine and
John Sease

LANDSCAPE ARCHITECTURE
Mike Kaiser, Kaiser Trabue
Landscape Architecture

Pages 249–251
On the entry facade, the central block's verticality
contrasts with the humble scale of two asymmetrical wings
that embrace an intimate garden. Dressing up
and dressing down simultaneously, the house combines
rustic fieldstone walls, formal cut-stone columns, and
a wing resembling an English cottage.

Pages 256–257
With low-sweeping shingled roofs, deep porches,
and a rambling asymmetrical form, the rear of the
house assumes a relaxed country-house charm.

RETREAT, Page 258

ARCHITECTURE
Bobby McAlpine and
David Baker

INTERIOR DESIGN
Susan Ferrier

Page 259
Telephone poles and an industrial table are among
the many nonresidential elements found throughout
this house.

Pages 262–263
Softly upholstered furnishings provide an island of
understated luxury amid rustic wood surroundings.

Pages 268–269
Drawing from the language of exterior architecture, the
interior of the lakeside pavilion combines shingles with
crisply painted moldings. Surrounded by dark shingles, the
white frames of the arches accentuate the sublime view.

ASCENSION, Page 272

ARCHITECTURE
Bobby McAlpine and
Scott Torode

LANDSCAPE ARCHITECTURE
Mike Kaiser, Kaiser Trabue
Landscape Architecture

Pages 271–283
Combining glass, thatch, and rubble stone, James's Well
marries the permanent with the impermanent, the
rustic with the refined. Its unfamiliar pairing of earthy
simplicity and symbolic geometry invites you to approach
with a sense of wonder.

ACKNOWLEDGMENTS

This book would not exist without the vision, talent, and generosity of many people, especially the homeowners who walked the path of inspiration with us to find the poetry of place. These shared imaginings could not have been transformed into reality without the boundless skill and industry of our design family in Montgomery, Nashville, Atlanta, and New York. Along with partners Greg Tankersley, Chris Tippett, John Sease, David Baker, Ray Booth, and Susan Ferrier, I thank you all, as well as the skilled builders and artisans who artfully translate our ideas into three dimensions. Many thanks are also given to those who worked together on the writing, design, and publication of this book, including Richard Norris, who touched every detail with precision and care, and coauthor Susan Sully, who brought passion and understanding to our collaboration. Special thanks go to Rizzoli International Publications' senior editor Sandy Gilbert Freidus, publisher Charles Miers, consultants Jill Cohen and Lizzy Hyland, graphic designers Doug Turshen and David Huang, and Kris Kendrick for her assistance with our vast photography library. Together we have brought this book into being. Finally, much gratitude is offered to the photographers whose artistry captured our work so beautifully and the magazine editors who have shared it with the world.

ABOVE: The partners of McALPINE (from left to right): Bobby McAlpine, David Baker, John Sease, Greg Tankersley, Susan Ferrier, Ray Booth, and Chris Tippett.

PHOTOGRAPHY CREDITS

Caroline Allison: pages 82, 115, 118–119, 132, 134–135
Jean Allsopp: pages 68–73, 74–77, 79–81
Mali Azima: pages 225–237
Roger Davies: pages 213–223
Erica George Dines: pages 33–49, 87–103, 287
Pieter Estersohn: pages 67, 78, 116–117, 120–131, 133
Roger Foley: pages 202, 204–211
Emily Followill: pages 259–271

Laurey Glenn: pages 238, 240–247 (Courtesy of Southern Living)
Tria Giovan: pages 184, 186–193
Eric Piasecki: pages 2–3, 5, 9
Simon Upton: front and back covers, casewrap, pages 6, 13, 14–31, 51–57, 59–65, 104, 106–113, 136, 138–149, 151–169, 171–183, 249–257, 273–275, 277–279, 281
Peter Vitale: pages 194, 196–201

DRAWING CREDITS

David Braly: endpapers, pages 84 (with Greg Tankersley), 85
Scott Torode: pages 276, 280

First published in the United States of America in 2017
by Rizzoli International Publications, Inc.
300 Park Avenue South
New York, New York 10010
www.rizzoliusa.com

2017 2018 2019 2020 / 10 9 8 7 6 5 4 3

Printed in China

ISBN 13: 978-0-8478-6034-0

Library of Congress Control Number: 2017942296

Project Editor: Sandra Gilbert

Editorial Assistance: Hilary Ney and Elizabeth Smith

Production Manager: Barbara Sadick

Art Direction: Doug Turshen with David Huang

Endpapers: South African Cape Dutch, Flemish, and modern styles are fused in this design for a house in South Africa.

Pages 3–4: Residential poetry can occur most dramatically in places that seem unintended for human habitation. The entrance to this all-wood cottage is reminiscent of a carriageway to a courtyard for watering horses.

Page 5: A cupola illuminates the interior of an outbuilding in a compound in Tennessee. Gathering light, it also emits light like a lantern. From a poetic standpoint, this is what helps you find your way.

Page 6: With a parapeted Flemish gable and a Tudor-style ogee window, this house has stylistic origins that are both familiar and hard to trace.

Page 9: Larger than openings found in residential architecture, the arched apertures of this house call to mind a carriage house or stable. Wide glass doors look as though they might fling open to the light of the courtyard at any moment.